P9-BJO-071

COOKING WITH CANNABIS

QUICK AMERICAN ARCHIVES

Published by Quick American Archives
Oakland, California

Copyright ©1999 Bobcat Press

ISBN 13 # 978-0-932551-30-6

This book contains information about illegal substances, specifically the plant Cannabis Sativa and its derivative products. Quick American would like to emphasize that Cannabis is a controlled substance in the U.S.A. and throughout much of the world. As such, the use and cultivation of Cannabis can carry heavy penalties and may threaten an individual's liberty and livelihood.

The aim of the publishers is to educate and entertain. Whatever the publisher's view on the validity of current legislation, we do not in any way condone the use of prohibited substances.

Printed in the U.S.A.

 Contents

Practiced for thousands of years in the East, sadly, cannabis cuisine is a neglected art in the western world. Although an hour in a hot kitchen can hardly compete on convenience with rolling a joint or filling a pipe, swallowing your pot does have genuine advantages...

When cooked in large doses with the right ingredients, cannabis can create the kind of high normally associated with powerful psychedelic drugs like L.S.D. For some people this is an attractive prospect. Even at lower doses, the unique qualities of a cookie high make it a worthy alternative to smoking. Variety, as they say...

Another incentive to eat rather than smoke are the obvious health benefits. Some joints are rolled with the 'demon' tobacco, and cannabis smoke, though less damaging, still contains tar and other nasties. By eating your pot you can get high *and* avoid inhaling all those carcinogens. For non-smokers, (who may not be able to inhale properly) and sufferers of respiratory problems, eating is an easy, pain-free way to enjoy cannabis.

Discretion is another good reason to get cooking. While pungent clouds of blue smoke are a bit of a giveaway, nothing looks more legal and less narcotic than a cookie. A tub of cannabinated butter or a jar of hash cookies is a subtle and discrete way to store cannabis. For people using pot medicinally, cannabinated food, with it's longer lasting effects, allows them to avoid the (potentially awkward) task of smoking several doses throughout each day.

Cooking is also an excellent way to make good use of pot you wouldn't want to smoke. Cannabis leaf, which is low in THC and harsh to smoke, is often treated as waste

by domestic growers and discarded or given away. When cooked into food, dirt weed, trash hash and low-strength leaf will give a kick on a par with that from the best flowering tops.

Instead of simply presenting a collection of recipes using pot, this book attempts to explain the whole process of preparing, cooking and eating cannabis. Whether you want to spend 5 minutes knocking up a hash yogurt or a week brewing up a high-powered THC concentrate, *Stir Crazy* has the answers.

The simplest way to eat cannabis is to stuff it in your mouth and start chewing. Bad idea. Aside from the unpleasant taste, eating 'raw' cannabis creates a slow-acting and unpredictable high. Dissolved into fat or alcohol, the active ingredients, or *cannabinoids,* in cannabis become easier to digest for a much better, more intense high. This is the basis of all cannabis cookery.

This chapter explains some of the more useful techniques in cannabis cuisine. You'll learn how to prepare cannabis, how to mix it with other ingredients and how to make high-powered THC concentrates. There's no need to get involved in the complexities of cannabis science to bake the perfect brownie, but a few basic principles will stand you in good stead. Follow the three golden rules and all will be well...

Rule

Use Fat or Alcohol

Once dissolved in fat or alcohol the active ingredients in cannabis pass much more quickly and completely into the bloodstream. This means a better high in a shorter time, using less cannabis. Hurray! Most of the recipes in this book contain a high proportion of butter or margarine—your friendly, fatty passport to a good time.

Rule

Keep it Bite-Sized

For a fast, effective high, cannabis should be eaten in small amounts of food. A full stomach will delay, prolong and weaken the effects of eating cannabis. More food in the system means less cannabinoids reaching the bloodstream, and they'll take longer to get there, too. For this reason, most of the recipes in this book are for snack-sized foods. The munchies should be left till later.

Rule

Watch the Dosage

Never 'guess' amounts when adding cannabis to food. Dosage accuracy is vital for a good experience. Get it wrong and either nothing will happen or you'll be sick as a dog. You *can* overdose on cannabis and everyone has a horror story about the 'spacecake' that drained every drop of blood from their sorry face. Always follow the dosage table on page 17 (it's easy!) and be very aware of how much you are eating.

What to Use

Leaf

Leaf is sold cheaply or even given away by growers who often regard it as little more than waste. This is good news for the cannabis chef, as leaf is a perfect cooking ingredient. Although unpleasant to smoke, the large amounts needed to get high are easily condensed into a single, tasty cookie. Properly cooked leaf will get you just as high as the best buds from the same plant.

Bud

Although they represent less value for money than leaf, the flowering tops of the plant still make an excellent basis for cannabis cooking. Because of its higher potency, only small quantities of bud are required, making for a less obtrusive cannabis taste.

Hashish

Hashish is perhaps the easiest of all the cannabis forms to cook with. Much of the preparation has already taken place during its manufacture and hash is easily dissolved in fatty foods. Hash can simply be crumbled into most recipes. Because the potency of cannabis solids can vary so wildly, a degree of caution is advised when deciding hashish dosage.

The Other Bits

The stalks and stems of the cannabis plant contain a small amount of THC. This is best extracted using alcohol (see page 17) as the material is too fibrous and bulky to be used directly in cooking. Cannabis seed husks (not the seeds themselves) are quite potent and can be used in the same ways as the flowering tops.

Preparation
Making Cannaflour With Leaf

The easiest way to prepare cannabis for cooking is to process it into a flour that can be added directly to recipes. Leaf for flour should be dry and crisp enough to be crumbled between your fingers. A short stretch in a warm oven or a minute or two in a microwave will dry fresh leaf.

1. Remove any stalks or woody debris and place the leaf in a food processor.

2. Process the leaf into a flour-like powder and leave it to settle for a minute or so.

3. Using a knife, work the cannaflour through a sieve to break down stubborn leaves and remove any remaining debris. You might notice a fine dust being thrown up during the process. This is precious, potent stuff, rich in THC. Don't let it escape. Cannaflour should be stored in an airtight container and refrigerated.

Bud Flour

Flowering tops can be made into flour in exactly the same way as leaf. If the bud is not crisp and dry, it should be warmed in an oven (200°F) for ten minutes or microwaved for a minute or so and then left to cool. A coffee grinder is more suitable than a food processor when using small quantities. Special care should be made to avoid losing the THC dust.

Hash Flour

This is simply powdered hash. How you make it depends on the consistency of the solids you are using. Most hash crumbles easily when heated —a minute or two in a microwave or a quarter of an hour in an oven should do the trick. A fine cheese grater or a mortar and pestle can be used to powder particularly hard hash. Very sticky, oily hash, such as Nepalese, can be chopped into tiny pieces with a sharp knife and added to the recipe—it will dissolve easily when cooked.

Bud Puree

Bud can be mixed directly into the liquid in a recipe. Ideally, the liquid should contain a high proportion of fat, milk, or alcohol.

① Break up the bud using sharp scissors, remove any woody bits and place the clean bud in a food processor with the liquid. Puree well together.

② Simply add the cannabinated liquid to the other ingredients in the recipe.

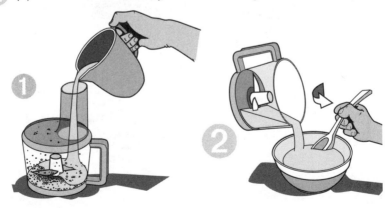

Using Milk

Both dairy and soya milk are excellent for cooking with cannabis. They contain an emulsifier called Lecithin. Lecithin distributes fat evenly throughout the milk, allowing it to dissolve the cannabinoids more efficiently, especially over heat. Even low fat milk will work well.

Making Cannamilk

This process uses milk to extract the cannabinoid goodies from cannabis. Sweetened with a little honey, *cannamilk* can be drunk as is, flavored to make a mind-bending milkshake, or substituted for normal milk in virtually any recipe.

Bring four cups of milk to a boil and stir in the cannabis. Both hashish and cannaflour will work fine. One dessert spoon of leaf flour (see page 17 for equivalents) will stone four people.

Cover the pan and simmer gently for at least half an hour.

Finally, use a coffee filter, or a fine sieve, to strain the milk into a container. If you don't mind your milk a little green and gritty, you can skip this step and the mix will be more potent. The finished cannamilk should be refrigerated and used as normal fresh milk. It can be frozen for longer storage.

Finally, use a coffee filter, or a fine sieve, to strain the milk into a container. If you don't mind your milk a little green and gritty, you can skip this step and the mix will be more potent. The finished cannamilk should be refrigerated and used as normal fresh milk. It can be frozen for longer storage.

Using Butter

Butter (or margarine) rules the roost when it comes to cooking with cannabis. It's versatile, tastes good and can be used in more recipes than your dog's had hot dinners. More to the point, cannabinoids dissolve easily in butter, especially over heat. Blended well with cannaflour, or powdered hash, it can be substituted for normal butter in your cooking. It can also be used to make a high-powered THC concentrate called *cannabutter*.

Making Cannabutter

Butter can be used to extract the active ingredients from cannabis for cooking. Cannabutter is potent, potent stuff. The THC from two ounces of cannabis leaf can easily be condensed into a single cup of butter.

Heat three cups of water in a pan. Add two ounces of cannabis leaf and half a pound of butter.

Bring the mixture to a boil, then cover the pan and simmer gently for one and a half to two hours, stirring occasionally.

3 Strain the mixture through a sieve and collect the liquid in a bowl. Use the back of a spoon to press the liquid from the leaf.

4 Boil two cups of water and pour it over the leaf to wash through any remaining butter. Repeat step three.

5 Strain the mixture through a sieve and collect the liquid in a bowl. Use the back of a spoon to press the liquid from the leaf.

6 Boil two cups of water and pour it over the leaf to wash through any remaining butter. Repeat step three.

Cover the bowl and refrigerate the liquid. When fully cooled, the cannabutter will harden and separate from the water. Scoop out the butter and store it in the fridge. The water can be discarded. Cannabutter can be substituted for normal butter in virtually any recipe. You can even spread it on toast.

Using Alcohol

Cannabinoids dissolve easily in alcohol, like vodka or gin. The higher the alcohol content, the better it works. Cannabis can be left to soak in a bottle of liquor for a couple of weeks to make potent, cannabinated booze or processed with alcohol to make a high-powered THC concentrate.

Making an Alcohol Concentrate

Making a THC concentrate with alcohol is a simple and useful way to process large amounts of cannabis leaf into a small amount of liquid.

1 Wash the leaf in lukewarm water. Drain, then place the leaf in a large, shallow bowl. Stir in a 750 ml bottle of spirit (cheap, strong vodka works well).

Ensure that all the leaf is submerged, then seal the bowl with plastic wrap and leave it to sit somewhere safe for two to three days. During this time the alcohol will extract most of the goodies from the leaf.

Remove the plastic, stir the mix, then leave it exposed to the air for a day or so to allow the alcohol to evaporate. About half the liquid should remain.

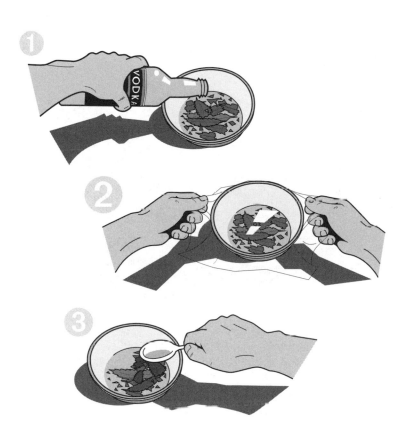

4 Stir the mix again, then pour it through a sieve and into a bowl. Using the back of a spoon, firmly press the remaining liquid from the leaf.

5 Pour some of the liquid you collected back through the leaf and press once more. Repeat this process several times to extract as much juice as possible.

You will be left with about a half of a cup of cannibinated liquid. This can

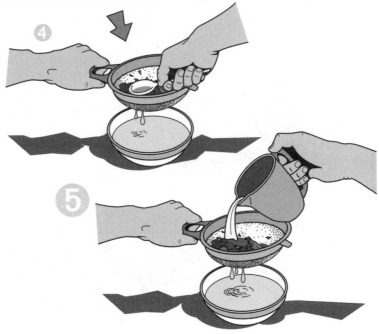

be further simmered down to an quarter of a cup. It should be bottled and refrigerated for storage. The extract can be added to a drink, mixed into food or taken as is. Beware, this stuff is superstrong. Prepared using the amounts described, less than one teaspoon of concentrate will provide a strong single dose.

ookie highs can be overwhelming and intense beyond the normal smoking experience. It is possible to become very stoned (sometimes too stoned— see *Overdose*) by eating cannabis. Properly prepared, even low-grade pot has the potential to send you into orbit. Because of this, pot in food deserves real respect from both the cook and anyone eating it. Whether you are looking for a mild medicinal effect or a full-blown psychedelic adventure, getting the dosage right is vital to having a good time. Eating too much is a common (but easily avoidable) mistake that can really spoil your day.

This chapter explains what happens when cannabis is eaten and how to judge the right amount to use. A little bit of common sense combined with some basic knowledge will ensure you avoid the pitfalls. Skip the following pages at your peril...

What Happens When You Eat Cannabis?

When cannabis is eaten, THC and the other cannabinoid compounds that create the high enter the blood stream via the digestive system. This is a slower and less predictable process than when cannabis is smoked. Whereas smoking produces an almost instant high, the effects of eating can take anywhere between 15 and 90 minutes to arrive. The time taken for the high to come on is affected by the way the food is prepared, the ingredients used and the amount of food passing through the digestive system at the time.

Soon after being swallowed, the cannibinated food reaches your stomach. Once inside the stomach, it is churned around in a mixture of acid and enzymes. Now liquified, the food is squirted, bit by bit, into the intestines. There, more enzymes and bile work on the fats in the food and the cannabinoids are absorbed, through the intestinal walls, into the blood stream.

Once in the blood stream, the psychoactive compounds are on a high-speed tube ride to the brain. Usually, within 45 minutes of swallowing some of the cannabinoids will have reached neural receptors in the brain and the user will begin to notice effects. As more and more of the chemicals make their way through the system, the user will become stoned.

The peak of a cookie high is generally reached within two hours. In some cases (after a particularly large meal, for instance) the effects can last for as long as eight hours. If you are taking a large dose, don't make immediate plans to visit the in-laws. The process of digestion changes the make-up of the cannabinoids and first-time cookie eaters are often surprised at how different the feeling can be to smoking cannabis. With large doses, many report an intense psychedelic experience with spatial distortion and sometimes even hallucinations.

Controlling The Dose

Whereas the joint smoker can regulate dose instinctively from toke to toke, the cookie eater must calculate amounts very carefully as nothing can be done after the food has been swallowed.

Put simply, being in control of the dose means having a good idea of the effect each cookie (or whatever) is going to have *before you eat it*. To do that you need to know the strength of the stuff you have used and the amount contained in the food. This may seem blindingly obvious, but it's all too easy to forget.

The dosage table opposite provides a *basic idea* of how much cannabis you will need to get the results you are looking for. It can only be an approximate guide because the effects of eating cannabis depend on so many factors. Body weight, metabolism, mind state and the previous experience of the user all affect the way they will feel, as will the quality of the cannabis and the way it is prepared. ➤

Dosage Table *

(handwritten) pleasantly stoned

(handwritten) In touch with God (use extreme caution)

(handwritten) A strong buzz

		pleasantly stoned	A strong buzz	In touch with God
POWDERED HASH	★★★	x 1/16	x 1/8	x 1/4
	★★	x 1/8	x 1/4	x 1/2
	★	x 1/4	x 1/2	x 1+
BUD FLOUR	★★★	x 1/8	x 1/4	x 1/2
	★★	x 1/4	x 1/2	x 3/4
	★	x 1/2	x 1	x 1 1/2
LEAF FLOUR	★★★	x 1/3	x 2/3	x 1
	★★	x 3/4	x 1 1/2	x 2+
	★	x 1	x 2	x 3+

★★★ Leaf and bud from professionally grown 'nederweed' strains such as Snow White, Northern Lights, etc. Premium, finger-made hashish, such as Pollen.

★★ Good, compressed bud. Lower leaves from potent plants. Good street hash.

★ Low grade or dirtweed. Lower leaves from inferior plants. Poor street hash.

* All measurements are in level teaspoons (roughly equivalent to just over a gram in most cases) and are based on a reasonably experienced user weighing 160 pounds. The recipes in this book assume the use of medium-quality (two star) bud flour. When substituting hashish, leaf or other bud, use the table to find the equivalent amounts. A test smoke will give you an idea of the strength of the weed you are using.

➤ Underestimating the power of cannabinated food is a common mistake (with unpleasant consequences) that can be easily avoided. The big message is to stick to the low doses until you are confident of the results. If you end up with weak, wussy cookies you can always eat a couple more until you get where you want to go.

Overdose

Cannabinated food can make you as high as a Himalayan kite on a long string, but it also has the potential to ruin your evening. While one too many 'Dutch strength' joints might reduce you to a drooling mess, one too many turbo-charged cookies could have you making friends with the porcelain in your bathroom.

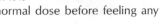

Because the effects of inhalation are felt almost immediately, the smoker can easily recognixe the signals when enough is enough. This is much harder to do when cannabis is eaten. Once cannabinated food is swallowed, the cookie eater is past the point of no return and committed to whatever high is on the way. It is possible to consume many times the normal dose before feeling any effects, making overdose a real danger.

Remember that time when you were 13 and you snuck out and drank an entire bottle of tequila under the bleachers? Do you remember how it felt just before passing out in front of the principal, with the rank taste of vomit on y our breath? Well, add a few unpleasant hallucinations of giant slugs chewing on your face and that's pretty much what can happen when you dig too deep in the cookie jar. The symptoms of overdose include nausea, dizziness, anxiety, panic, paranoia, rapid heart beat and an all over, deep rooted feeling of shittiness. Very commonly, the overdoser will fall asleep—sometimes for more than a day.

There are no recorded deaths from cannabis overdose and you'd probably have to work your way through a truck load of brownies to even get close to doing any permanent harm, but one thing is for sure: eating too much will make you feel really bad, if only for a while.

Avoiding Overdose

Easy! Just err on the side of caution when deciding 'How much?' If one cookie doesn't give the required kick then you can always eat a couple more. Remember that when eaten, pot has a more powerful and lasting effect than when smoked and the high can take up to two hours to peak. Cookie eaters with common sense wait an hour or so before 'upping' their dose—you never know if that 'meeting your ancestors' high is just around the corner.

Because cannabis potency can vary so much, a little careful experimentation is an excellent idea. If you haven't cooked with a particular batch of pot before, follow this procedure: smoke a sample to get an idea of the strength; use the dosage table (page 17) to work out the approximate dose; *eat half that dose;* wait an hour or so to see how you feel and then eat more as required.

Although many experienced cooks measure ingredients 'by eye,' cannabis warrants judicious accuracy in the kitchen. A dash too much chili powder might have you reaching for a cold beer, but too much leaf flour can leave you flat on your back while the room spins wildly around you.

Eating cannabis in combination with other drugs can give rise to some unpredictable, potentially nasty effects and should be avoided. Floating your pot with a lot of alcohol is likely to make you feel sick. It's best to leave any boozing for an hour or two after you have eaten.

If Things Go Wrong

Aside from steering clear of roller coasters, heavy machinery and people in uniforms, there really isn't much you can do during overdose. You just have to sit it out. Find somewhere warm and womblike, curl into the fetal position and reflect on your foolishness.

There is a psychological element to most cannabis experiences, and what some might appreciate and enjoy, others may find worrying and unpleasant. If things do go wrong, chill-out, stay calm and remember that while you may have a radically distorted reality and feel as sick and dizzy as a rollercoaster-riding wino, you are in no real physical danger. Even during the most extreme cannabis overdose the human body functions without problem physically. Cannabis is one of the safest psychoactive substances and conventional medical wisdom assures us it would take an unfeasibly vast amount to do anybody any lasting physical harm.

The worst part of any overdose should be over within an hour of first feeling the effects. After that, if you can stay awake, the experience is likely to become much more manageable and enjoyable.

The following recipes are tried-and-true favorites. All contain high levels of fat or alcohol to aid in the digestion of pot, and all are bite-sized to hasten absorption. This is quick and easy stuff, even for the most virginal of chefs and can usually be ready to eat in under an hour.

Stir Crazy is a guide to cooking with cannabis, rather than just a recipe collection. If you haven't already, read the first two chapters. Using the techniques described you can put pot into thousands of different recipes—any good cookbook will give you plenty of ideas. *Stir Crazy* uses cakes and cookies as the basis for its concoctions because they are good to eat in small quantities, but anything from pot pizza to cannabis casserole is possible.

Remember to store cannabinated food out of the reach of children and pets to ensure that it isn't eaten by mistake.

Ingredients

Flour

Plain flour only is used in the following recipes. Don't get it confused with *self-raising flour,* which contains raising agents and can create some unpredictable results. As a healthier alternative, *wholemeal flour* can be substituted for plain in most cases. If you are using large amounts of leaf flour remember to reduce the amount of normal flour accordingly. All flour should be sifted to remove lumps before use.

Fats

A vital part of most cannabis cookery, fat dissolves the active parts of the pot. Although butter gives the best final flavor, margarine works fine in baking and is a good option for vegans. Soft margarine is particularly good as it can be blended easily with pot straight from the fridge.

Eggs

Allow for the fact that eggs come in different sizes. The following recipes are based on large eggs. Eggs should be stored at room temperature (refrigeration can spoil them) and ideally used within a week of purchase.

Sugar

Normal granulated sugar can be used in most recipes. Castor sugar is finer and dissolves more easily giving a better texture, but is more expensive. Some recipes may demand soft brown or demerara sugar.

Chocolate

Cannabis and chocolate always seem to go well togeth- er. The brown gold is also very handy for hiding the greenish color that results from using large amounts of leaf flour.

Equipment

Oven

These vary, so the times and temperatures given are approximate only. If you have a fancypants convection oven, remember to reduce the times appropriately. When you are baking, resist the temptation to take a peek before its time—opening the doors unnecessarily creates heat loss and can spoil the finished result.x

Baking Tray

These need to be greased and lined. Using a paper towel, apply a light, even coating of butter (or whatever fat you are using in the recipe) to the tray and then line it with greaseproof paper. The paper should also be greased with fat.

Wire Cooling Tray

Once baked, cakes, cookies, etc. should be left to cool on a wire tray. This allows air to circulate and  stops things from sticking or becoming soggy.

Weighing Scales

These can be inaccurate, especially with small amounts, so it is preferable to use a teaspoon or electronic scale when measuring pot. A proper set of balance scales are best for measuring other ingredients, but any reasonably precise scale will be better than guesswork.

Palette Knife

A cheap and useful thing to pick up at your local cookery store, a palette knife is very handy for spreading and smoothing mixtures and removing cakes and cookies from the baking tray. In a pinch, a broad, blunt knife or spatula will do the same job.

Electric Mixer

Last (but definitely not least), a blender or electric hand whisk is invaluable in cannabis cookery. It is vital to spread the pot evenly throughout the food in order to get reliable results, and a couple of minutes with a mixer is worth ten with a hand whisk or spoon.

Adding The Pot

Dosage is by far the most important part of making good cannabinated food. Your cookies might taste like insoles but if you get the dosage right, the chances are that they'll do the job. Likewise, no matter how good your brownies are, if you put too much (or too little) pot in them you ain't going to have the fun you want. The dosage bar shows how much pot to use in each recipe. Here's how it works:

This is the amount of cannabis to use. Each spoon represents *one level teaspoon* of cannaflour (ground-up pot) made from medium-grade bud shown on the dosage table with two stars. If you are using another kind of pot, check the table (page 17) to get an equivalent amount.

Use: 5x 🌿 Makes: 20   One Cookie is One Dose

This is the number of cookies to make. It's really important to get them all the same size so that the doses are uniform.

A quarter of a level teaspoon of two star bud flour should get you pleasantly high. Five divided by 20 equals one quarter, which is one dose. Simple, eh? At the risk of sounding pedantic, always experiment with a half dose first, so that you know what you're letting yourself in for.

Couch Cookie

M ost cookie recipes work well with pot—the classic couch just happens to be one of the favorites. Buttery nuttery nonsense, easy to make and ready in under an hour.

Use: 5x 🌿 **Makes: 20   One Cookie is One Dose**

3 oz. Plain Flour (75g)

4 oz. Butter (110 g)

4 oz. Soft Brown Sugar (110g)

1 Large Egg, Beaten

½ tsp. Vanilla Extract

2 oz. Toasted Chopped Nuts (50g)

Prep. Time: 15 minutes
Cook Time: 25 minutes

Pre-heat Oven to: 300°F
(150°C)

Beat the cannaflour, butter and sugar together in a mixing bowl or blender till the mixture is light and fluffy.

Now, beat in the egg and the vanilla extract, add the remaining ingredients and stir until thoroughly mixed.

Scoop up lumps of the cookie dough, roll them into ping-pong ball sized rounds, then arrange them on baking trays. Allow plenty of space as the dough will expand in the oven. Flatten the balls into cookie shapes.

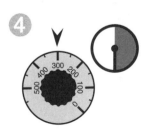

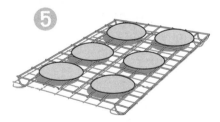

Bake your cookies in the center of the oven for about 25 minutes, or until they become golden brown and feel firm to the touch.

After baking, quickly transfer the cookies onto a wire rack to cool. Store the cookies in an airtight container.

Freefall Flapjack

Just like Grandma used to make—with an extra kick. Get your salivary glands oozing for an ear-popping plummet into oaty awesomeness. Mmmm . . .

Use: 2^1/2 🪂   Makes: 10   One Jack is One Dose

4 oz. Butter (110g)

4 oz. Brown Sugar (110g)

2 tsp. Golden Syrup

6^1/2 oz. Oatmeal (175g)

1 tsp. Ground Ginger

Prep. Time: 15 minutes
Cook Time: 45 minutes

Pre-heat Oven to: 300°F
(150°C)

Place the cannabis, butter, sugar and golden syrup together in a saucepan over a low heat. Gently stir until the butter has melted.

Remove the pan from heat and thoroughly mix in the oatmeal and ginger.

Pour the mixture into your baking tray and press it out evenly (about an inch deep) using your hands or the back of a large spoon.

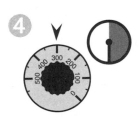

Place the tray in the center of the pre-heated oven and bake for 45 minutes or until golden brown.

Once baked, remove the Jacks from the oven and leave to cool for 10 minutes before cutting into individual pieces.

fearsome fudge

Sticky, scary stuff. A couple of chunks of fearsome fudge is just enough to give your friends a treat. Works best with hash or cannabis extracts. Yum, Yum . . .

Use: 3 ³/4 🌿   Makes: 30   Two Fudges are One Dose

½ cup Condensed Milk (150ml)

½ cup Milk (150ml)

4 oz. Unsalted Butter (110g)

14 oz. Castor Sugar (440g)

¼ tsp. Vanilla Extract

Prep. Time: 10 minutes
Cook Time: 45 minutes

Throw all the ingredients into a saucepan with a good, solid base and stir the mixture over a low heat until the sugar has completely dissolved.

Turn up the heat and bring the mixture to a boil. Continue boiling until the mixture reaches a temperature of 250°F (120°C) on a sugar thermometer.*

Remove the pan from the heat. Stir the fudge vigorously for about 4 minutes and then pour it into a greased tray.

When the fudge has cooled and almost set, cut it into 30 equal squares with a sharp knife. Once completely cooled, wrap in greaseproof paper and store in an airtight container.

*If you don't have a sugar thermometer (jeez, amateurs!), then keep boiling until the mixture starts coming away from the sides of the pan. Drop a little of the fudge into a glass of water. If it forms a soft ball when it hits the water, then it's time to take the pan off the heat.

Badman Brownie

Chocolate goes with cannabis like cheese on a cracker and these good 'n' gooey brownies are no exception. Tried, trusted and easy to make.

2 oz. Plain Chocolate (50g)

4 oz. Butter (110g)

2 Large Eggs, Beaten

6 oz. White Sugar (180g)

2 oz. Plain Flour (50g)

1 Level tsp. Baking Powder

¼ tsp. Salt

Prep. Time: 15 minutes
Cook Time: 30 minutes

Pre-heat Oven to: 300°F (150°C)

32

Break the chocolate into small pieces and place them, together with the butter and cannabis, in a basin over simmering water.

Keeping the heat very low and gently stir the mixture until it has melted. After beating the eggs, stir in the remaining ingredients.

Pour the mixture into a baking tray and spread it out evenly using the back of a large spoon.

Place in the center of the oven and bake for 30 minutes. The brownies are ready when a knife inserted into the mixture comes out cleanly.

After baking, allow the mixture to cool for ten minutes or so, before cutting into squares. Transfer the brownies to a wire tray to finish cooling and then enjoy!

Crucial Cookies

*C*hocolate and herb combine to make these cookies a crucial treat. If you have a high tolerance for chocolate, double the dose of chips. Then sit back and enjoy the gooey goodness in every bite.

Use: 5x 🌿   Makes: 20   One Cookie is One Dose

3 oz. Plain Flour (75g)

4 oz. Butter (110g)

4 oz. Soft Brown Sugar (110g)

1 Large Egg, Beaten

$\frac{1}{2}$ tsp. Vanilla Extract

3 oz. Chocolate Chips (75g)

Prep. Time: 15 minutes
Cook Time: 25 minutes

Pre-heat Oven to: 300°F
(150°C)

Beat the cannaflour, butter and sugar together in a mixing bowl or blender till the mixture is light and fluffy.

Now, beat in the egg and the vanilla extract, add the remaining ingredients and stir until thoroughly mixed.

Scoop up lumps of the cookie dough, roll them into ping-pong ball sized rounds, then arrange them on baking trays. Allow plenty of space as the dough will expand in the oven. Flatten the balls into cookie shapes.

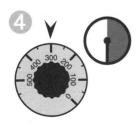

Bake your cookies in the center of the oven for about 25 minutes, or until they become golden brown and feel firm to the touch.

After baking, quickly transfer the cookies onto a wire rack to cool. Store the cookies in an airtight container.

Short Cuts

Don't have the time or equipment to cook from scratch? Simply can't be bothered to slave over a hot stove? Thank your lucky stars—pot is easily added to many ready-made foods. The results will be much the same and you'll have more time to enjoy.

Baking Mixes

A quick scan of the shelves in any supermarket will reveal dozens of ready-made baking mixes for cakes and cookies. These are ideal for cannabis cookery. Most call for added butter and this is a good way to introduce the pot. Simply chuck the butter and cannaflour into a food processor, mix it thoroughly and use as directed.

Sauces

Powdered or canned sauces and toppings are another easy route for kitchen slackers. Pick one with loads of fat or milk, then simply blend in cannaflour over a low heat. Canned stews, soups and other savory stuff with a high fat or milk content can be used in the same way. You'll get better results if you mix the cannaflour into a paste with a little oil before adding it to the food. The lower the fat content, the more time you'll have to allow for the cannabis to dissolve.

Using Hash

Hash is the speed king of cannabis, and also possibly the convenience queen. Solids don't need processing and dissolve quickly and easily in fat or alcohol.

An often used camping trick is to pour a little oil into a metal spoon, crumble in the hash and then gently heat it over a flame. Once the hash has dissolved, the oil can be stirred into yogurt or hot chocolate (or any milky drink) and then consumed. Try to do the spoon and flame trick somewhere private—unless you get off on looking like a cheap extra from a 'Just Say No' After-School Special.

Quick Firewater

Well, maybe not quick exactly (you'll need to leave it a w   h   i   l   e   ) but it only takes a couple of minutes to actually make and a   l   l you need is some pot and a bottle of booze. Gin, vodka, whisky—you can use pretty much any spirit with over 40% volume (80 proof) alcohol. Open up the bottle, break up the weed, drop it in and voilá! The bottle should be resealed, then left somewhere dark and safe for at least a week (the longer the stronger), by which time the booze will have absorbed most of the THC and other goodies. You should aim for one dose to one measure of spirit, as too much booze with your pot will make you feel bad.

TV Dinners

The microwave, see how it glows? It is your friend.

Nuke your food for half the allotted time, add pot, then nuke for the remainder. Again, the high fat/high milk content rule applies, so avoid any cuisine that's lean.

*C*annabis has enjoyed a symbiotic relationship with humankind for over 8,000 years. The plant has been cultivated all over the globe and for many years was the world's most common crop. Cannabis has been called 'the most useful plant in the world'—here are a few of the reasons why.

Getting High

There are records dating back to 2737 BC of cannabis being used for its psychoactive effects in medicine, recreation and religious ceremonies.

When ingested, THC travels into the bloodstream and then directly to the brain, where it targets brain cell receptors linked to memory, emotion and coordination. In 1992, a naturally produced neurotransmitter—*anandamide* (a name derived from *ananda,* the Sanskrit word for bliss)—was discovered to target the same receptors and mirror the effects of THC.

A socially acceptable drug in the nineteenth century, it is only recently that cannabis has suffered under the hard hand of the law. Sparked by the (now laughable) rantings of a few 'moral' speakers and fueled by lobbyists fearful of the burgeoning threat of hemp to their oil, cotton and timber industries, cannabis prohibition caught fire in 1930s America.

Incorporated (under U.S. pressure) into the international drug laws, cannabis soon became illegal throughout most of the world.

Manufacturing and Industry

Cannabis is a highly versatile resource. The Business Alliance For Commerce In Hemp has so far recorded over 50,000 commercial uses for the plant. Environmentalists and forward-thinking industrialists alike point to cannabis as a feasible and entirely sustainable substitute for fossil fuels and lumber. It can be used in the production of paper, textiles, construction materials, plastics and even petroleum. This is no revelation. Up until the nineteenth century, hemp was the world's number one crop. It provided the lifeblood for global commerce, war and industry. Even as late as WWII, the US government ran a campaign to encourage farmers to grow cannabis for the war effort.

One reason cannabis is such a uniquely valuable plant is because of the fibers contained in its stems. These can be woven into strong, durable fabrics; made into rope or processed into a pulp which is similar (and in many ways superior) to wood pulp. Incredibly, one acre of cannabis will produce as much pulp as four acres of woodland.

Cannabis is also an excellent source of cellulose—the starting point for the production of organic plastics. Unlike plastic made from petrochemicals, plant-based plastics are bio-degradable and carry a lower environmental cost.

Although it is hard for the oil-fueled psyche of the twentieth century to grasp, it is perfectly possible to produce fuel from plant material. Hemp is one of the best sources of biomass fuel. Had history followed a different course we could well be filling our cars with hemp-sourced fuel.

Cannabis hemp is, in many ways, the ideal environmentally friendly resource. It grows easily, even in poor soil, virtually anywhere in the world and requires few damaging and expensive pesticides. Unlike fossil fuels, it actually consumes carbon dioxide and produces oxygen, thereby fighting the greenhouse effect. A global economy based on plant matter rather than fossil fuels would spread wealth, phenomenally reduce pollution and provide a lifeline for developing countries blessed with perfect growing conditions. Cannabis has deep, far-reaching roots and these are

Incorporated (under U.S. pressure) into the international drug laws, cannabis soon became illegal throughout most of the world.

Manufacturing and Industry

Cannabis is a highly versatile resource. The Business Alliance For Commerce In Hemp has so far recorded over 50,000 commercial uses for the plant. Environmentalists and forward-thinking industrialists alike point to cannabis as a feasible and entirely sustainable substitute for fossil fuels and lumber. It can be used in the production of paper, textiles, construction materials, plastics and even petroleum. This is no revelation. Up until the nineteenth century, hemp was the world's number one crop. It provided the lifeblood for global commerce, war and industry. Even as late as WWII, the US government ran a campaign to encourage farmers to grow cannabis for the war effort.

One reason cannabis is such a uniquely valuable plant is because of the fibers contained in its stems. These can be woven into strong, durable fabrics; made into rope or processed into a pulp which is similar (and in many ways superior) to wood pulp. Incredibly, one acre of cannabis will produce as much pulp as four acres of woodland.

Cannabis is also an excellent source of cellulose—the starting point for the production of organic plastics. Unlike plastic made from petrochemicals, plant-based plastics are bio-degradable and carry a lower environmental cost.

Although it is hard for the oil-fueled psyche of the twentieth century to grasp, it is perfectly possible to produce fuel from plant material. Hemp is one of the best sources of biomass fuel. Had history followed a different course we could well be filling our cars with hemp-sourced fuel.

Cannabis hemp is, in many ways, the ideal environmentally friendly resource. It grows easily, even in poor soil, virtually anywhere in the world and requires few damaging and expensive pesticides. Unlike fossil fuels, it actually consumes carbon dioxide and produces oxygen, thereby fighting the greenhouse effect. A global economy based on plant matter rather than fossil fuels would spread wealth, phenomenally reduce pollution and provide a lifeline for developing countries blessed with perfect growing conditions. Cannabis has deep, far-reaching roots and these are invaluable in preventing soil erosion—an enormous problem in parts of

I n short, yes. Virtually all the valid scientific studies point to cannabis being an incredibly safe substance. That is not to say that cannabis cannot do harm. Any drug can have adverse effects when abused or overused and pot is no exception. Extensive research and thousands of years of anecdotal evidence have given us a good idea as to what cannabis does to the mind and body.

Short-Term Effects

Cannabis is unusual in that it produces effects similar to those of many different psychoactive substances. The drug does not easily slot into any of the normal psychoactive groups (depressants, stimulants, hallucinogens) and displays characteristics distinctive to all three. A group of people using cannabis may swing from introspective states of dreamy detachment to high-energy conversation and collective euphoria.

The short-term effects of cannabis use are largely dependent on the quality of the substance and the individual's mood, personality and previous experience. Studies show a marked difference in effects between 'first-timers' and 'veteran' smokers. It seems that with repeated use, a user learns to anticipate, recognize and enjoy the effects while an inexperienced smoker may just feel confused and dizzy. Environment and company also influence the experience. For instance, subject X eating cookies in a room crowded with strangers might experience paranoia and fear while subject X eating identical cookies in a room with a few close friends might feel particularly relaxed and at ease.

PLEASANT SHORT-TERM EFFECTS

Some of the more common subjectively positive experiences include the following (often in this order):

- Euphoria and/or a feeling of general well-being
- Uncontrollable hilarity (or 'the giggles')
- Increased sociability and talkativeness
- Enhanced perception of colors, music, art, nature, wallpaper, etc.
- Increased mental energy, lateral thinking and creativity
- Major changes in consciousness (dude)
- Distortion of time and space
- A ravenous appetite (or 'the munchies')

UNPLEASANT SHORT-TERM EFFECTS

Negative subjective effects, more common among new users, may include the following:

- Forgetting what one was saying, thinking or doing, often in the middle of saying, th ... Err, sorry, what was I saying?
- Paranoia—often related to the fact that the user is aware they are breaking the law
- Anxiety and confusion
- Fatigue and drowsiness
- Losing your keys

Cannabis and Driving

Any drug that affects perception will also affect the ability to drive, and cannabis does have an adverse influence on driving performance, especially when used in high doses or when combined with other drugs. However, the results of a comprehensive study (carried out in 1996 by the U.S. National Highway Transportation Safety Administration) shows that driving impairment from cannabis use is far less serious than that caused by alcohol use and is comparable to the effects of many 'over-the-counter' medicines.

Long-Term Effects

For such a widely-researched drug, a lot of controversy and confusion still surrounds cannabis and its long-term implications to users' health. Studies have been repeatedly debunked as politically-motivated scaremongering or just plain old, bad science. Many of the flaws in the investigations revolve around their failure to relate to the actual use of cannabis in 'real life.'

In truth, there is little sound evidence to suggest that long-term cannabis use singularly causes significant physical or mental health problems. An examination in *The Lancet* (11th November 1995) concluded: "The smoking of cannabis, even long-term, is not harmful to health." Others disagree, so let's take a look at some of the claims relating to long-term effects on the human mind and body.

Long-Term Effects on the Mind

There is no doubt that cannabis has a profound effect on the mind during intoxication, but arguments of enduring effects are hotly contested. A complicating factor is that, as cannabinoids stay in the body for up to fifty days, there is a danger of residual effects being confused with permanent damage or change.

Motivation

The occasional forgetfulness and lethargy (the so-called *amotivational syndrome*) that affects some heavy cannabis users seems to be dependent on continued use and/or the personality of the individual. Much of the thinking surrounding amotivational syndrome is rooted in the '60s, when the establishment viewed cannabis as a primary cause for social unrest and deviancy. There is no evidence at all of an enduring effect after use is discontinued and many heavy users lead complex and busy lives without any apparent difficulty.

Memory Loss

Short-term memory loss (as in 'what was I doing just now?') is a well-known symptom of cannabis use. However, there is no evidence to suggest that this a permanent, or ongoing, effect.

Dependence and Tolerance

Cannabis is often described as a 'non-addictive' drug. However, as with most drugs (including tea and coffee) an element of social or psychological dependence is possible for some users. Cannabis 'habits' tend to be based more around the simple desire to repeat a pleasurable experience than real compulsion. Problematic addiction that seriously interferes with a user's normal life seems to be very rare indeed. Surveys show that most cannabis users stop in their late twenties.

Anecdotal evidence suggests that tolerance to the effects of cannabis does develop with continued use, although it is possible that this is due to users adjusting to, and learning to cope with, their inebriated states.

The 'Stepping Stone Effect'

In the absence of any strong health or behavioral arguments, anti-pot campaigners tend to dredge up the old 'stepping stone' or 'gateway drug' routine. The premise of this appears to be, that while it *may* be fairly harmless, smoking a joint (or munching a hash cookie) is just the first step towards puffing on a crack pipe and selling your grandmother's best china for skag. This is tantamount to claiming that drinking the odd glass of wine is a slippery slope ending under a railway bridge with stained pants and a bottle of meths.

If, for a moment, we accept the logic of the gateway argument—that taking mild drugs leads to taking hard drugs—then where exactly is this gateway? Does the buzz from strong coffee lead to a thirst for gin and then on to a craving for PCP, or what? Does Redbull™ lead to amphetamines? Should we ban strong mints? The only truth in this argument against legalisation arises from the fact that cannabis is banned in the first place. Because it is an *illegal drug*, buying cannabis brings you into contact with *illegal drug dealers*, who by definition sell other *illegal drugs*, which you might just be tempted to try.

MENTAL ILLNESS

Claims that cannabis can cause serious mental illness have been common ever since the 'Reefer Madness' propaganda of the 1930s. In fact, there is no evidence to show that lasting mental disorder can be directly caused by cannabis. Whether the drug may trigger a latent illness, or make worse/improve an existing one is open to question, as there are a myriad of everyday elements in a person's life (relationships, health, work, etc.) that have that capability.

Long-term Effects on the Body

RESPIRATORY DISEASE

The smoke from an *ital* (pure) cannabis joint delivers three times more tar than your standard cigarette, more than five times more carbon monoxide, and hits the throat and lungs at a higher temperature. This has lead some experts to declare that, blow-for-blow, cannabis smoke is more likely to cause respiratory disease and cancer of the lungs, throat and mouth than tobacco smoke. One study has shown an increased incidence of throat cancer among cannabis smokers. Other experts point to evidence that respiratory cancers are largely caused by the radiation present in tobacco tar and maintain that the carcinogenic nature of cannabis is wildly overstated. In any case, comparison with tobacco should be tempered by the fact that a twenty-a-day habit of unshared ital joints is relatively rare.

There is no conclusive evidence that moderate cannabis use leads to significant damage to the respiratory system. However, the standard tobacco/cannabis joint must (at least) carry the same risks as an unfiltered cigarette. Avoiding the possible danger of respiratory disease is easy: do it the *Stir Crazy* way and eat your pot instead.

CENTRAL NERVOUS SYSTEM

Both reputable and highly disreputable sources have put forward the claim that cannabis causes brain cell death. Such claims are highly controversial and no permanent effects have ever been demonstrated in humans. Whatever the truth of the matter, there is no evidence to suggest that the 'possible' damage causes any significant change in behavior or mental performance.

REPRODUCTION

Bizarre claims that cannabis reduces libido, causes men to grow breasts, and disrupts menstruation in women have been circulated since the sixties. You won't be surprised to hear that (yet again) there is no scientific basis for these claims.

Male cannabis users do produce a higher proportion of two-tailed spermatozoa which tend to be too confused to make it to the ovum. Coffee drinkers also experience this phenomenon and cannabis users will be relieved to know that there are usually millions of the single-tailed variety ready to step in and do the deed. In any case, the genetic coding of the sperm is not affected.

IMMUNOLOGY

There is some evidence, both real and anecdotal, to suggest that cannabis use may have a slight, temporary effect on the body's immune system. There is nothing to show that this possible effect is more significant than that suffered with moderate alcohol or caffeine use. Much of the evidence may originate from contagious diseases (especially the common cold) hitching a ride on joints passed between friends.

Is it legal?

Estimates put the number of regular cannabis users in the United States between ten and fifteen million, with more than one in three young adults thought to have tried the drug at least once. Using cannabis is now common outside of its traditional sub-cultural environment and is seen as increasingly acceptable throughout most of society. Whether this trend will continue is another matter and, for the time being, cannabis is still very much a controlled substance with users running the risk of prosecution and harsh penalties.

Cannabis and the Law

U.S. drug law is infamous for being tough on offenders. You need only consider the *War on Drugs* of the '80s and mandatory minimum sentencing of the '90s to know that drug users and growers must tread carefully to avoid detection by authorities.

FEDERAL AND STATE LAW

Cannabis laws can vary from state to state and sometimes conflict with federal laws. For example, California now allows the use of cannabis for medical purposes, but federal agents continue to seize paraphernalia used to grow or distribute cannabis, even when it is grown for use as a medicine.

Confused? You soon will be. When it comes to breaking the law with cannabis, there is plenty of scope.

Of course, the best advice is not to get caught, but just in case, get to know the consequences of cannabis use in your state. Your local NORML chapter is a good source of information.

USE/UNDER THE INFLUENCE

Driving under the influence can lead to loss of your license and jail time. Being involved in an accident while under the influence makes you entirely responsible, even if the other driver was at fault.

POSSESSION

Possession can include possession of cannabis, or possession of paraphernalia for use in the sale or trafficking of cannabis. The penalties of an amount of cannabis for personal use vary from state to state. If you are suspected of trafficking or selling cannabis, the authorities have the right to seize any or all property suspected to be used for trafficking or selling the drug, and any assets purchased with profits from traffic or sales. This includes everything from weighing instruments, to your car, house, or your bank account. Be very careful not to incriminate yourself as a dealer.

SUPPLY

Supply, a.k.a. distribution, a.k.a. sale, a.k.a. trafficking, can range from passing a joint to importing tons of hashish. The guidelines on sentencing for trafficking are based on a sliding scale relating to the offense and amounts involved. Custodial sentences are common at the mid- to high-end of this scale.

As with possession, there is a group of offenses which can be listed as trafficking: *possession with intent to supply*—where there is evidence that the amounts found are not purely for personal use; *offering to supply*; *conspiracy to supply*; etc.

CULTIVATION

Needless to say, growing cannabis in the United States is illegal without government permission, or—in California—without the recommendation or prescription of a physician (and then, only for personal use). The real problem for growers arises when the amounts are significant in the eyes of the law and attract additional charges of intent to supply or trafficking. As with possession and supply, strong mitigating factors can come into effect if the substances found are deemed to be for personal or medical use, but again, be aware of the limits imposed in your state to avoid incurring additional charges which can result in long prison terms or seizure of property.

Other Implications

Conviction for a cannabis-related offense can leave you with more than just jail time. Due to a number of laws, institutional practices and societal attitudes toward drug users in general, the consequences of a cannabis conviction can be far-reaching and may include the following:

1) Being excluded from particular careers—employers don't look kindly on drug convictions;

2) Public humiliation—local newspapers (especially those of the small town variety) love a drug story;

3) Being banned from driving if convicted of driving while under the influence;

4) Refusal of bank loans or credit if convicted of supplying or intent to supply;

5) Refusal of immigration requests and even temporary visas for work or holidays by some countries;

6) Possible difficulties with fostering or adoption proceedings and, in some extreme cases, the removal of children into care.

SELF-PROTECTION

The best advice for avoiding prosecution is, of course, not to commit an offense. Social acceptance of cannabis use in youth culture and sub-cultures can lead to an over-casual attitude toward the drug. It is worth bearing in mind that over 85% of cannabis-related convictions are for simple possession of cannabis—not for the sale or manufacture of the drug. The second-best advice for avoiding prosecution is to be very, very careful. Being charged with offenses more serious than justified is sadly a common occurrence. Weighing instruments, a divided stash or large amounts of the drug can mean a charge of intent to supply rather than one of simple possession. Helping out your friends, especially on a regular basis, can be a risky business.

Suspicion of cannabis possession is frequently given as a reason for police to stop and search, and suspicion of supplying cannabis allows authorization for search warrants and seizure of property.

If you are arrested by the police, the best advice is to know your rights. Do not admit to an offense or otherwise incriminate yourself before obtaining the advice of a lawyer, to which you are entitled by law.

Grow with Ed

MARIJUANA
GROWER'S HANDBOOK

Ed Rosenthal provides the most accurate and up-to-date information on the best strains, equipment, and methods for increasing potency and yield. This book will change the way you grow.

500 pages of full color photos and illustrations show how to maximize your crop. No matter your goals or your level of experience, this is the book to have.

Official Coursebook
Oaksterdam University

Ed Rosenthal's ASK ED™ Library

Changing Marijuana Policy
One Book at a Time